Pomegranate

You are a pomegranate.
dark crimson flesh, each piece of you, hiding a seed of thought.
You are a pomegranate.
camouflaged in a sea of kings and queens,
never really given a chance.
You are a pomegranate.
When you are cracked open, they will realise the layers and layers you are composed of,
a symphony,
a richer metaphor than an onion.

If you give them a small, sweet taste of yourself to them,
they will be enticed for more.
And one day they will declare:
"You are exquisite!
From your hard exterior, to your exposed, inner juicy thoughts.
You are worth more than the mangosteens and durians before you."

But my dear-
I have always known this about you.
That your tiny seeds will bloom into forests,
creating a whirlwind of crimsons, just like you.

Because you?
You are a pomegranate.

A letter to my tics

As the day progresses,
you emerge.

Sounds ominous, I know: I'm trying to see you as a pet. A creature I never asked for, but was given to.
And like a Christmas present from a distant Aunt,
I've sympathetically adopted you into my body. You live in me now.
the quick spasm of brain to mind to blood vessels to nerves, a jerk, a shock, an electrocution-
it's almost like a dance.
Well, if you consider a dance like one of a Caucasian dad attempt of sorts but fast forwarded way too quickly, so fast but so adamant it's hard to miss.
and I laugh in embarrassment, because I don't want to love you.
I don't want to glorify you,
Or keep you,
Or protect you.
But when you bark inside of my body I cannot help but react.
So, I will let you stay in my home of a body until you pass away.

And you will come and go,
and maybe,
I will grow.

Second letter to my tics

Okay. Time to stop.

I know you're excited, but you're turning me into a one-woman musical, a jukebox that won't stop singing.

And I know you mean well but I really didn't ask for a surprise party,

So, when you whistle and click I feel like I'm harassed by you.

This is hard- I said it before.

But you are not a joke anymore, you are painful and in me and please, creature, sleep.

Because if you do not, I cannot as well.

The pins and needles in my head jerking and clicking and flicking- are driving me insane.

So, my creature. I do not want to label you as a monster, because that will give you power.

So,

When will you fade?

I shall be waiting.

OCD

The air is thick but I am breathing

It's like everyone was born with gills,

Or a bubble around their head

And I'm the only one trying to breathe

Or a robot is taking over me;
Left

Right

Left

Right
Left

Right

OCD is a virus and I am its slave

A host sounds powerful but I am none of these things

OCD is a death, and it's preparing my grave

But I am not ready

For any of these things.

OCD is terrible,

I want to shoot myself I say;

But I am not selfish,

No,

I am none of these things.

OCD can go fuck itself.

Right Way Around

Red and white

The cars stream

Left and right

The cars swerve

Black and blue

My eyes are bruised

Up and down

Where my headspace is

Up and down

And left and right

Where my death trap is

Up and down

And left and right and all the way around my head and back through and right up and left to-

Death reaper awaits

Maybe It's a Tuesday Thing

Maybe it's a Tuesday thing,
I get up and start the morning

Maybe it's a Tuesday thing,
How could I ask for one more?

Maybe it's a Tuesday thing,
I never wanted these sensations,
Tingling,
Heavy breath,
Whizzing blackness.
Remains of regurgitated lunch down the toilet,
I'm so confused
Why is this happening to me?

Maybe it's a Tuesday thing,
I get up and start the morning

A Conversation

You say, "My pleasure",

Which is simultaneously the most selfish and selfless phrase said;

I don't know which one is your intent.

Jen

Apple tea with cinnamon please

Or a HCM at 12 am

You are an owl, a tortoise, a living breathing human

A metaphor, a statement, an everything in between

You are my favourite person to chat with

In a café filled room with empty coffee cups and singing discs

A soy chai tea latte please

Or a HCM at 12 am

Dear Whimsical

You teach me how to grow,

Tell me,

How did you learn to love yourself?

You should be written in the bibliography of every book

An unknown credit of every person you meet

A changing force, a soul who sees beyond the ego

You don't give about things that don't matter

A hermit in the paint splattered room, hiding, but also so
So
So

Unafraid

Of the realm between life and death.

Tell me,
How did you become so wise?

You are a spinning lovely in a world full of pounding.

Brighter than all,

Depth beyond all,

You've earnt my respect faster than the speed of light,
The light you so happen to be
In the universe you know so intricately,

Analyzing it like a piece of art.

Tell me,

How did you manage to live on this strange, beautiful mess of an earth?

Growing Pains

You laugh and I laugh,

Our stomachs stretched like balloons about to pop.

It's how we know

We're having growing pains.

Trace

I think I knew when I used to sketch backs,

And they all turned out to be the backs of girls.

The way it curves and flows,

The trapezium bone jutted out slightly.
Trace it down the spine,

Like a wave.

And I trace and trace it again,

Accompanied by fluttering eyelashes,
Whispering in the corner of sunlight in June.

Every single time,

my heart beats so hard,

I can feel it drumming away trying to escape.

It's pulsing out my chest,

Beating to the rhythm of my breath.

I don't understand,

And I don't think I ever will.
But right now,

I will sit here in the sunshine,

And quietly continue

To sketch backs.

Pull Back the Bow

My brain is a target practice,
And the arrows are my worries.

My heart is filled with shopping bags of nothing,

How can I buy entities when my price tag reads zero?

My soul is a necklace,

One meaning to decorate but instead chokes.

But I got out,

I did,

And I'll do it again.

My brain will fire up and shoot bullets through the arrows,

My heart will fill with golden specks of treasure,

My soul lifting up and stabilizing my structure, no longer just a trinket.

I will balance again,

And not be afraid.

For I am the arrow of a target practice,

And happiness is the bullseye I am aiming for.

It Is What It Is

Because life is a game,

And everyone is a player.

We just so happen to be playing on different sides.

What You Are

"She is a storm cloud",

They say.

But they forget clouds change shapes in the split of a second,

A beautiful creature a child would point at.

"She is competitive,"

They say.

But I know you are only so because you need to.

That you inhale fires, exhale oxygen,

Steam bygone,

Creating something beyond yourself.

"She has attachment issues,"

they say.

But I know you won't give up something worth loving.

And you are worth more than what anyone tells you.

Peek

You speak in rubber band language.
A hit or miss inspiration in the midst of blabbering.
You fill the room with laughter,
A fluidity people breathe into,
Becoming high on the drug that is you.

There is something I can't quite put into words-
How everyone seems like shells of themselves,
Compared to your intactness of your inner being.

And you who inspire,
With polo thrifted outfits,
And eyes darting around the corners of the sphere,
You see something so beautiful in your spirit.
I could only wish to take peek.

Fine Line

Medicine is just legal drugs,
And dependency is inevitable.
Who cares about prescriptions?

Pop the pills.

What a fine line between good and bad,

What a find line I am crossing.

Confidence is just underrated arrogance,
Why have a black market when I'm selling away my organs?

Seems like a waste of secrecy to me.

What a fine line between good and bad,

What a find line I am crossing.

Tell a story right and it will be twisted,

Faded into the line between rumour and truth.

What's wrong with a white lie?

What a fine line between good and bad,

What a find line I am crossing.

Promise

Calm, anxious heart,
Heaven hears your whispered prayers
The wind blows in all directions
And with leaves whirling around you, I will lift you home.

Calm, saddened soul,
Heaven had your foetus enwreathed in your mother's womb,
Woven in bands of gold and silver
You are my precious creation

Rest, my love,
Realise my grace
I promise I will protect you always
For You are mine and I am yours
Never forget my promise to you.

Habitat

Positive psychology program says:

'Take intrusive thoughts less personally, and let go of your emotional reaction to them.'

But how can I let go of

Go shoot yourself, go shoot yourself, go shoot yourself, again and again and again?

Stop.

Get out of my head.
Go stab yourself,

My brain says.

Stop.
I can't stop the constant whirling of noise, not a white noise, oh no, that would be too simple. It's like a multi-coloured, ever changing fucking NOISE taunting me, everything moving too fast and I can't stop it.

Stop. Please stop.
I fear even glancing at my body, let alone showering. Because I can't see myself naked, flesh and all, like

toy my brain wants to play with. It's too painful.

It's gnawing at me, eating me inside.
All I want to do it rid of this day. Get rid of the intrusive thoughts and let them go. But they feel like someone stamped them on me, when I wish they were stickers that I could peel off me. Pluck the blood sucking thoughts out and throw them away.
But they are leeches, they're alive and how do I do I take them off me and let them live in another

habitat?

Please.
Let go of me?

Thanks, Janey

I don't understand why everything hurts,
My body doesn't feel like my own.

Lurching forward,
Jittering, flinching, tripping, shaking-
Shit.
Sidewalks and stairs seem like a cruel joke right now.

You prop me up and look me into my eyes.
But I can't see you properly under my blurry, dripping vision,
So, you grab my hand and hold it tight.
Tighter, I'm trying to grasp for your fingers.
It just feels numb.

I can't hear the ambulance wail,
Because the pain in my head is screaming.
So, I listen to your voice instead,
Like a calm steady heartbeat.
I don't feel like I'm cracking into pieces anymore.

My love,
You are so much stronger than I am.

You are a stable rock in my glitching presence,
And I am so grateful to be your friend.\

Salute Your Fists

Salute your fists in solidarity,

In rebellion of mediocracy,

Because all we need is responsible capital,

Instead of agreeing with the political animals.

Salute your body for reality,

In anger against the Monarchy,

Because we need frustration,

To reverse our countries' deflation.

Salute your soul a little stronger,

Shout and scream for a while longer,

Because now is time to take action,

When our Governments' are amidst distraction.

Lord, my God

In some realm or another
We are creations of the Father
Created to reject sinners,
Attempts to be glorious winners

But we failed, time and time again
Lean in, unravel your chain
Human shape takes its form
Listen to the light, not mankind's scorn

Life breathes into itself,
Ready for the king,
Bring Him back to earth

Gramps

The world is sinking without your green ship

sailing

The liminal phase

Where are you now?

Acaracow

It is morning,

And We tuck into the bed that's too small for two people

Giggling about the past day.
The world is calm, unwilling to be worried in this moment.

She sighs in amusement, watching us squander in bed before the sun rises.

It is afternoon,

And we are running across roads,

The red light glaring.

(Well, you are, while I stand in shock like a rigid rock;

How can I move while the passing cars are streaming?)
You stand on the other side and laugh,

Rolling your eyes.

You do not believe in death.

It is night,

And we sit together in silence.

We are exhausted, not of each other but of the day.

So, we sit and sit and go back to bed that's too small for two people,

Until the world feels calm again,

And the sun rises the next morning.

Viewing

The universe does not see you as your authentic self.
You,
Well,
You are a wisp, an amalgamation of peaceful depth
A truth beyond meaning,
even if I just made that up.

Because according to the dictionary,
Your name is under the word 'butterfly'.
There is not a speck of regret in the way you glide
I wish I breathed in the same air as you do,
To have the same understanding of space as you.

Because you are dark silver matter,
Embedded golden shadows,
Peeking through the brightness of the relentless sun.

If I could pinpoint you as a shape,
You would be a soluble, cynical, shattering escape
Slipping through my fingers
I can see you smile already

You are a dragon fruit,
A joy,
An everything you want to be

But I could be oh, so very wrong
You could be none of these things
Because I have everlasting faith in your unsolvable presence.

So, let the universe see you as anything they want you to be.
You'll be perfectly untouched.
I just know it.

Sea crabs

My sister once said:

"There are crabs nipping on your feet."

I don't think I ever plucked the crabs off.

I just let them nibble,

Gently acting as the prey

Watching the cycle of life unfold before me.

Surprise me

You are a burst of confetti,
An exclamation mark,
A roller coaster that only goes down

You are an unfinished piece,
A never-ending chatter
A skip in every 2 steps

Pens and papers are your fortunes
Your heart never stops soaring to rhythm of your boots
Splashing in the rainbow oil spills,
Laughter like gold

Thank you for reminding me of innocence

A curatorial rationale

She is her own exhibition.

Her clothes, a canvas of snipped away fabric. Tucked in to her jeans.

There is no colour scheme.

The face represents defiance, intentionally drawn to mimic an 80's cartoon character. There is no stopping her.

Human texture. Emulated after latex.

A range of oils always plasters on the crevices of her knuckles. They look red, like she's been in a bar fight with herself.

Post 2019 Tse art.

On a good day

There is light spinning through the creases of your eyes.

You are a peaceful ocean,

A stillness beings watch in the warm hue of a morning.

There is depth in your waves,

A lapping shore of rhythms,

Breathing living seeking human being of the love that you gave.

You are the embodiment of eyelashes,

Underrated luckiness

But you are not delicate,

No,
You are the strongest ocean I've ever met.

Sinking feeling

I am a blanket, a comforting purpose that hasn't fulfilled

Because how much love can a blanket give when it's too hot under, it's too heavy, it's too much?

You tell me not to blame myself

I wish you were right

Tongues of the voices

I

The dichotomy between the ways our tongue clicks is so great.

The language curls up in balls, caught in our throat. What do you have to say for yourself?

II

In tongues, they allow themselves to lift up high, a God ridden kryptonite of the future. A synopsis of what is to come.

III

There is something quite beautiful in the way you speak. But like a pondweed frozen in a river, my tongue can't fit into place into the jigsaw of words I want to express.

IV

Mouths open wide, stretching until there muscle aches in awe. Tongue jutted out slightly. There is nothing brighter than the light stand of the dentist. No words are needed.

V

Silence.

Space

There's a bridge that connects my home to yours

Where there's a ray of lingering sunlight,

A birdsong of the ages

A lifter of the drifting might

You hummed along the tune

The other day I was walking

There was a road sign reading

'No trespassing

No strangers

No fucking asshole suffocators'

Sinking, breaking, dissipated longing
A croaking melody

A muttering ramble of wronging

You stood up, got going,

Don't leave

Tomorrow they will start building a site

In the middle of the space between you and I

I can only watch

Fears

I am not afraid of being scooped out of my pearls

Giving away all my capsules in my body of a vending machine

Offering solace in little crumpled papers, tucked inside strangers' pockets

But,

I am afraid of becoming selfish

That I already am selfish

Without knowing my true intentions

I don't know where I stand

I can't stop thinking about 5 pm when I staggered out of the house propped up against your arms and we left the fuse of a house open to the ambulance where it suddenly went silent except for the tics escaping through my chest into the void of the empty space

Diagnosis

I am not my diagnosis.
I am a complex, million celled organ of a human shaper shifter,
an anomaly of creatures,
a glowing tangle
Pale red creases on my sickle celled knuckles have underestimated my power to ignore them.

My diagnosis won't dictate my life.

Begin

My new psychologist has tics.

He told me to ignore them,
His eye rolls without distain,

His coughing without disease

I shook his hand in respect,

My neck cracking without annoyance,

My hand flicking without harm

I know we'll get along

Lightning Source UK Ltd.
Milton Keynes UK
UKHW042017060820
367821UK00001B/55